MW00514292

BIG THICKET BLUES

Sundress Publications • Knoxville, TN

Editor: Erin Elizabeth Smith
Editorial Assistant: Jane Huffman

Colophon: This book is set in Adobe Caslon Pro.

Cover Image: Karina Nöel Hean

Cover Design: Kristen Ton

Book Design: Erin Elizabeth Smith

Author Photo: Toby M. Schaeffer

BIG THICKET BLUES
NATALIE GIARRATANO

[signature]

To Susan—
Hope you enjoy these
rather bleak poems, and
I hope your Texas experience
was better than mine!

Best,
[signature]

Santa Fe
8-16-17

ACKNOWLEDGMENTS

Many thanks to the journals in which the following poems first appeared:

American Literary Review: "Self-Portrait as a Boy in *A Musician Family*"
Black Tongue Review: "Swarm" & "Songs from Terezín"
burntdisctrict: "Surge"
Connotation Press: "Throat Circus" & "Thump"
Hayden's Ferry Review: "Asena, the Gray Wolf, to Tu Kuëh, after Many Years"
Isthmus Review: "Until the Bees" & "Harbinger"
Laurel Review: "To All the Sheep on Conic Hill, Balmaha"
Southern California Review: "New Coyote" (Winner of the 22nd Ann Stanford Prize)
Tinderbox Poetry Journal: "What Doris Kilman Couldn't Say to Elizabeth Dalloway"
Tupelo Quarterly: "The Translations"
TYPO Magazine: "Big Thicket Blues"
Welter: "Under a Texas Moon," "The Tap Dance Kid," & "The Other Side of the Bed," all originally published as *"La Via Vecchia"*

Some of the bracketed poems were published as a Leadbelly sonnet in *Beltway Poetry:* "Shiloh Baptist Church Cemetery, Caddo Parish." Some have appeared in their fragmented form in *The Zen Space*.

"New Coyote" was chosen by D.A. Powell for inclusion in the 2011 edition of *Best New Poets*.

TABLE OF CONTENTS

III.   The Bomb was Holy, Too

for C
and Z

I

First the Bodies, Then the Names

Swarm

~*after Virginia Woolf*

The weather tells me how wooden I am, belly down to read the tide, trying to dry myself out of this drifting; I am ten again in Galveston, not feeling guilty for ignoring the jellyfish on the beach, never entering the water because of who might be floating in it, who might brush her body—part flesh, part vegetation—against my skinny legs (never mind the science of decomp; there's always flesh); these days I know jellyfish are hardly breathing through prisms of oil, are like ovaries that men walk by with giant bags in which to collect them, to take them home, wash them off, string them into necklaces; these days I'd rather be stone.

[When did your mouth
stop swiveling its hips,
grounding out ragged
grains of truth?]

Big Thicket Blues

~for James Byrd, Jr.

1

Someone loves this between forest and jungle
Texas.

Its wild dogs and families full of grace.

Cradled in sycamore, cypress, willow and/or
pines that tower and point
with precision of sharpshooters' guns.

Men herded men, lumbered and oiled the shit
out of this land. *Spindletop*'s slick, wooden
bequeathal of refinery lung.

Ships slunk into this gulf for post-Civil
War slave delivery.

(Refine that.)

Hard winter never comes but brains are
squirrelled away anyway.

God soundlessly slithers in and out of a skull
like a water moccasin.

It's in my honey / it's in my milk.

It ran with me under pines until I could
pretend the fallen needles and cones no longer
hurt my bare feet.

2

A black man tore purse from shoulder and
phantom pain still slides down my mother's arm.

Her eyes bounce around like pinballs when
she runs into someone whose skin flashes her
back to that act.

Fangs, whiskers, and pointed ears inked on the
dark faces in my father's yearbook.

His own hard baseball face had only popped
a few red stitches.

He'd soon be pitched to
a brotherhood of electrical workers.

They made sure to put us kids in *Brady Bunch-*
only kinds of yearbooks.

Festival of liberty.

Jimmy into another life, or:
slip into the back pocket of what's left
of this thicket like the hi-hat slips,
nearly unnoticed, into song.

3

Some can't breathe in this dense in-between;
nothing's ever all that much alive alive-o
in these pines. Or it's too much.

When I sang (with bullfrogs) to my sisters at night—
first when there's nothing, but a slow glowing
dream—I only half-believed in sleep and song.

Electrician versus homemaker each night he was home,
all night long—not the Lionel Ritchie version.

I stayed awake for the clicking of small, brown
cucarachas across the linoleum
as he flicked the lights on.

(I can't be boy or nun
but maybe a secret closetful
of functioning antique rifles.)

Out by our pond where we jarred
tadpoles, skulls of dogs
perched on sticks.

That that kind of wicked
apprenticed in my neck
of the woods.

4

Citizens on sundown town's attempt at
desegregation, otherwise known as
Operation "fly in milk bowl:"

One woman on *Inside Edition* has a baseball
bat and is willing to use it on "niggers and
nigger lovers."

Another "don't mind being friends with them,
talking and stuff like that, but as far as
mingling and eating with them, that's
where I draw the line."

In chemistry class: can alchemy change blue
blood to gold? I considered this with cheap liquor
until almost blacked out.

5

Neighbors of fire: their cocksure teeth
gleamed in the sun like broken glass.

The Klan doesn't do the whole
clandestine thing anymore; no white robe/
pointy hat get-up in the dead of night.

From I-10, I saw them parade like some mean
kind of Mardi Gras; imagined chains and ropes
instead of purple, green, and gold beads
for a flash of black chest.

Local sheriff looked into the news cameras
and said, "There's no organized Klan in these
parts anymore," as though he was trying to
convince his kids that he still loved
their mother.

6

In college/flux,
when three cocksures chained you to the back
of their pickup as though you were some old
leather shoe—the kind people used to tie to
newlyweds' cars to ward off evil spirits—

I'd just changed my major from criminal
justice to communications.

Tongue-tied and dizzy.

When they ground you into gravel wasteland:
trail of flesh and limbs and face married to 75
different sections of road.

Cops circled each spot unceremoniously
in red spray-paint, spelled out "HEAD"
where it had been whipsawed from your body.

I wondered if my family full of grace saw criminal
or animal.

My obsession with JFK's assassination
waned.

On the six o'clock news one of your murderers
claimed: "I'd do it all over again."

So as not to forget this or to self-contradict,
he has mapped it out with ink on his body.

7

Your friends say you whooped whatever
piano was around.

Shook some Al Green tunes out of any
ordinary day.

On this magic road, you can be anything
you wanna be.

Like your favorite artist once again known as Prince,
you could pick up any instrument
and make it home.

And we sing, James: *Honey, I know I know I know*
times are changing.

They say you always knew you'd put Jasper,
that jewel of the forest, on the grand old
Texas map.

Fuck Texas and the mapmaker
who waits until you're three miles
wide to mark your spot.

Your kids *only wanted one* (more) *time*
to see you laughing.

I wonder if, out on that old logging road,
your song was sure and clear, lightning
in their veins.

Sometimes (always), the past erupts
out of the muck like a snake we didn't think
was there but is suddenly in our goddamned boat.

All shocked and appalled.

8

Up in Michigan, I still try to shake
thicket out of this sluggish
stumbling into myself.

Gulf marshes and levies recede through
no fault of their own; we'll soon know
all their secrets.

In a presidential election year, from telephone
safety, I call my mother
racist.

In Texas, just before Obama is elected,
Brandon McClelland is run down, dragged
underneath truck to his death.

"Fringe element," some townsfolk say.

Fancy talk for: we're already getting over
this road-burning away of dark bodies.

Easier to rehearse our alibis,
get to the local carwash,
clean this busted pickup of proof.

[We must understand the soft,
secret code tapped out like paper
cups clinking along cement. Share
memories of bombs in our bodies,
waking and killing and creating
a cancer. (While the pines
whisper to Jesus.)]

Self-Portrait as My Estranged Father

Of concern: I will be so tired
when I've run out of anger
that water will fill up my mouth,

and the words, slick as marbles,
I'll trace with my tongue as they
slide down the belly that refuses

to speak. But I'll hold nothing
against it. I'll be done
with that sort of thing.

: not enough Beatles songs to play
back-to-back to fill the time
after the body steps in—a last stand

to transfer everything it has felt
rightfully back to the brain all at once.
: not enough countries in the world

in which to find all of my daughters
who'll leave clues just so I can't
find them because, after all, I taught them

not to talk to strangers, the nowhere
men they can now sense years ahead
while time is busy dictating that I'll

always be at memory's table. : that it's
my job to keep me alive—I just can't
take the chance that someone will be

waiting for me at the bottom
of this slide. : that I'll mistake
myself for some crazy son

of a bitch and give him nothing but
a bullet by which to remember.
: not enough whiskey or beer

to keep this old heart drowsy—
if the heart is slow, so follows
the brain and body. : that all

of these years will need much
longer to overtake the levy
when the storm comes barreling through.

Night Doesn't Fall at River Orchy, Scotland

The light would never leave us. It was so bright in the highlands that I thought the Earth had forgotten its Globetrotter's trick or gotten caught up in unlikely galactic sap. But even if the sky had not kept me awake, the sound of the rapids rippled and crashed through our heads like bees riled up in a hive. Sisters in a tent with our husbands hid in that small, sighing part of the world, in the folds around lochs and wool of sheep, but in our bones we knew that daughters always come home. That more than sons, we pay the price for a father's dream— even the quiet, hard-lurking one in which he's a pro baseball player. We aren't allowed to be with these bodies. And I thought he really should have been a historian, could picture it as clearly as the shine on his books about the U.S. government, some of the presidents, all of the wars. And I think he'd really like the highlands, considering all of the bloodied earth beneath us. The Scottish seem to hate the British as much as I hope he hates himself. Anyway, there was enough of him with us that we should have tossed it into the river.

Surge

They say you can't take the thicket out of the girl, so bayou swells under the uninterrupted Michigan snow. When winter plucks the last reeds from my head, I pretend it doesn't hurt (sends cottonmouths crawling). This is the season for the danger in filling up too much—snakes have been known to crawl on roofs of flooded houses, fight for a spot to escape the dark humor of a hurricane. If you can cut through wood and shingle with muscle and axe—smoke screens: the sun declares rights to flesh. Burning is imminent anyway, and it all burns —snake bites, snow, the melting away of a mouth.

New Coyote

It's midnight in New Mexico, after who knows
how many noddings-off, CD changes,
and quiet tamale stands in Texas dust,
before we feel safe enough: hundreds of miles
from Johnson Space Center and the I-45
corridor, where Houston investigators
routinely interview the bones of schoolgirls,

plenty far from looming rock formations
when out of the tumbleweed along I-10,
howls find their way out—coyotes siren
for hours. They appear along the sides
of the interstate only to disappear into dry dark.
The Chevy moves on quickly, its instinct
to flee. It's the coyote's to chase us down,

it's mine to turn the car around—save us all,
as if they need saving, these neophilic creatures.
But maybe it *is* in my nature to go back,
to be amazed at its smallness, how voice can be
much bigger than body—like those of us
eight-year-olds who sang "We are the World" for seven
dead astronauts. They fell apart, their shuttle dissolved:
a cube of ice in the fevered mouth of the universe.

And I used to be able to fall asleep
by tree song, that familiar lull of rustle
and fidget in wind. Instead: chickens rip
open wide the air with squawks as coyotes
raid the neighbor's coop and schoolboys
pied-piper their prize-winning swine
to slaughter. How does this all work?

Coyotes showing up in subways and
elevators. That day. These newspaper
clippings. This looking back on it as though
terror had forgone the spark of city for sky,
and all the days since I've tucked inside
skin and sleep, partly existing, never awake
to becoming some small, wild dog that haunts
a desert it doesn't need any more.

[Do we: let the slim ghost
of our senses blues up our bodies,
bottom out until we've cooked
our fear and eaten it too?
Or do we: dance ourselves
into love in order to find
the language of all things?]

Asena, the Gray Wolf, to Tu Kuëh, after Many Years

1

I've dented the side of an iron
mountain with my head. What can

I say: out of frustration. Tried to
hide it with tree bark but, honey,

nothing hides itself well enough
once a whole empire has walked

out of a woman, this woman who
doesn't mind doing all the work

and respects that you are all torso
and pretty face and the father

of legions of limbs. But sometimes
I do wish I'd found you before they

removed your arms and legs
so I'd have something with which

to pin you down. These lupine muscles.
This longing for reciprocated touch.

I'm sure the flesh of your belly is some
divine window I have yet to learn

to look into at the people after us—
children with their hearts licked clean.

2

I sense this is all dissolving. The smell
of your skin on my fur is almost extinct.

Our bodies have stopped communicating.
No guts to spill, not even to spew.

Sometimes I think of the coldness of these
metal Altais. Mine and yours. So cold

with our lack of want for what gravity
owns. In this sedentary life you have no

choice but to claim, even storms that fly
down to us from the mountains

into these valleys of wasting away
are miraculous. The lightning awakens

instincts forgotten in this dale
with no memory that tries to erase

us with its silence—its slow, deep breaths,
its green sighs. But instinct eventually

comes back to me, like misunderstanding.
Say: *Loyal dog*. Where else could I be at home?

II

A Jukebox, Not a Coffin

[Some blues are never recorded. No lips
twisting with last hisses of air from a balloon.
Sometimes a woman is a walking jukebox,
songs swelling like magnolia in the skin,
in the skin, like heat in thighs.]

Clamorous Pauses Between Marquees and Parking Lots

~for Lynda Hull

How it is: one minute you're dancing, the next
you're flying. Smoke of applause and papers
blowing in the wind around a medieval
cathedral in the dissolving heart of Gotham.

Buttress this city with spit and mud and sky
the color of dirty needles, but rally against abandoning
blue of stain-glass windows, failed windows
that want to return to quartz sand like notes

from a sax want to curl back to creator. Hesitate,
shoeless, on buckled sidewalk. Black pool of dress.
This plunging architecture is the weapon that never
left. Light up from inside so that the place burns.

Poem for Crying Stranger in the Alley

Hush, little girl. Don't you know
it's past midnight? We all hear

you crying like you saw your
daddy's throat slit or Jesus

fall dead from the sky. If not
Jesus, Big Bird. Hush, little girl;

he doesn't really die. But nothing
really explains why you're

crying this way, a way I've
never, in thirty years, cried.

Even when I stayed up all night,
blankets over my head, trying

to muffle the sounds: the murder
weapon he almost made from a pillow,

him screaming the words
I was not allowed to say. I wanted

my sobs to be almost as smothered
as hers. But not you, baby girl.

No, you've gone and woken
the whole neighborhood with

that wailing. You just want
to go home, but you can't;

I just want to do something, but
instead, I sit at the open window

hoping somebody else might be
safe with you. Besides, what good

is this woman in a dark alleyway
at midnight? I might be lost like you.

Lost like the life you just left
but don't know you shouldn't want back.

Take it from me, little girl in the dark,
you don't want to be back in that

house just because the lights are on.

[Belly tight,
filled with iron
guts and bone.]

Under a Texas Moon

An old man graveled
Italian in my face as though
it would make me appreciate
whatever secrets were spilling over
from his decades of how to get the wife
back. (She always came back.)

He'd rattle on because I knew
some Spanish, which is *almost Italian*,
but he was too fast and loud
breathing from his nostrils.
In the 30s he hired someone to kidnap
his five-year-old son
from a new front yard.

(He always got her back.)
His hands on her face were never
tender like the songs he wrote for her:
Oh, Mary, Mary, who smelled like
newspapers left out in the rain,
spent her last eight waterlogged

years in a bed dancing with half
of a mouth. Her tongue would only
let her sing nonsense, but I knew
what she meant: she was already heavy
as the headstone he would refuse to buy.

The Tap Dance Kid

A boy ran moonshine underneath
a Missouri town and three fingers
on his right hand were missing—
the ones he'd claim were blown off

by fireworks—but all I could see was blade
exploding finger bones, flashes of blue
sparks in dirt, because he took too large
a cut for just a rum-runner; from then on,

he'd always be flipping everyone off,
even his great-grandkids, and we'd chuckle
at an old man's wrong-doing, look at our parents'
faces to see what they thought of it all—our washed-up

Tony Peanuts whose piano never minded
what he was missing when he played his
"Mariuch," mumbling in broken Italian
how that Elvis *rubato* his *canzoni.*

[Music thick with mud
and sweat: poultice for souls
at the bottom. Scrounge.
(Wait for the river.)]

The Other Side of the Bed

~for my paternal great-grandmother, Mary Blanda Giarratano
(1912-1994)

Forget to wake up
early and roll his cold ground
meat in your palms.

Throw the anonymity
of your dresses in the wash;
let the machine's motion remind you

how the violin's notes churn
in your hollow, and that there's never the need
to flirt with his piano. Forget the dark brick

of the restaurant's kitchen
walls through which you can hear
the impatience. Remember the world

only *seems* as though it's sealed
around you, that you could never drive
away from the soft voice with which

you loved your boys. Forget the women
who say you're to blame for their injustice
because you always follow his

breadcrumbs back. And forget
the God who never leaves you
any breadcrumbs at all.

[When there's no god to make flesh,
how a woman can marquee a feeling
that is the last minute of Earth.]

What Doris Kilman Couldn't Say to Elizabeth Dalloway

She wants you to think I'm the horrible
pollution in this city: fumes of my spinster's
muffler. Though, she's right in this: I do want
to fill your lungs and the space between
your legs. Never mind her bristling brand of spit-
shine when my hands shudder to be stars under
your telescopic gaze. Please have a seat again.
Who cares about wearing white gloves to bury
the milk of youth and eagerness and untapped
desire? Toss the Dalloway off and into the street
like the world has done to me. Let's live on periphery,
make our degenerate music. And know that if
you walk away right now, these hands are more likely
to be dying stars, heat folding in on heat until shadow.

[Sharpen your teeth on your own
bones and taste the body's breakdown:
involuntaries turn coward leaving
you with less than breath.]

Throat Circus

~for Malinda Markham

The finish line was glass.
Should've heard it shatter
long before thoughts flopped
and dried on the tile floor.

So easygoing about such
things. Collecting shadows
in another world, filling
their mouths with white

paint in networks of paper
flowers and lanterns that
would sooner float a grave
to sleep than glisten in wind.

Words are like cattle brands:
they don't feel obligated
for anyone to like the smell of burnt
hair and hide, only to feel anything,

much as the bone of life sticks
in a throat to throb out song,
so fast at the finish that muscles
of a heart have to multiply.

[Sometimes: funk in the blood-
stream or an ache that cracks
our plastic hearts; sometimes:
faces heavy with song after rain.]

Black Bear Shake-Up

If I took the shape of a thing
I've killed, I could navigate
this mountain unseen, make a less
blundering music as I crawl
unaffected by the bear in the tree
who's moaned in disapproval,
who may not exist if I don't look
up to see her, whose colorful scat
had me freaking out two miles up.
(*Don't say any of this out loud.*)

If I took the shape of a thing
I loved, I would lie to me about
noises in the woods, tell me that bears
won't bother us before finally admitting that
if the bear's only half afraid as I am,
we're toast, so keep moving, go slow
around the bend, make sweet, heavy-footed
music, sing our conversation but avoid
the song that reminds me of all of the places
we've never been.

No Condoms for the Heart

In which the lone wolf always
looks back to the place it has left.

In which halo of sundog
fences off an old crow or
shorthand for light is accidental.

In which more crows sprout
from loam to shine under the moon—
some other version of us who still polishes
rock, oils gun. Friction schemes.

In which we dance out of guns,
hover over each other's rivers as if
we're helicopters searching for body.

[Crows feast
on the dignity left. Shoo.
Give this a name before
survival's made meaningless
by holding close the tongue
like a poker hand.
(Wait for the river.)]

Harbinger

And the crows talk incessantly these days about how to murder the woman who, in taking her dog out for a shit, breaks up the lovely huddles in which they're planning (among other things) how to get a dead something-or-other out of the neighbor's garbage can; they must first distract the new world vultures that have ventured against urban lights and noise to this trash bin perch. Woman with dog changes her walking route but not before watching small crows swoop and peck at the predatory fowl as if they are the giants, as if they are heroes, as if they owned all rights to speak to the dead; they hold a vigil for whosoever happens to be in the bin, twist their heads closer to read the entrails: smoke rises from the woman's head, aching buries all in its black, but they do not even shiver.

III

The Bomb is Holy, Too

[The body begins
its entombing:
Gonna dance it into the ground.]

Stagnate

The body's song:
sometimes nearly
imperceptible even
when mouth of
a glass is pressed
to it, or when it is gloriously
slow like understanding
by two lovers after
a long fight. Darling,
seasoned animal
that doesn't skitter
off when it learns
even gods believe
in cancer. Heavy
oil and hair and sky
fall; faux stone speakers
pour out this white static.

Thump (on Frenchmen Street)

Real live trumpet cuts through my machinery—the glow of blue blood hiding in the secret room of a heart that (for now) is done playing dead; slide of trombone with a blonde girl behind it and all of us dancing because that's what souls waking up have to do (which supposedly sets us apart from other animals); then this guitarist—his back as stiff as the unlit cigarette in his lips but his fingers loose as slack rubber bands; funk curling into all the faces in the joint like an invisible smoke; an old, leathery woman who bangs tambourine to thigh, every now and then she blows the kazoo strung on a necklace that dangles on her breasts. If we all had a way to make some sense of each other through hot air and metal strings, arrangements of sound, rhythm of a life half-remembered, oh how this train that pumps its warmth into orbit around the tireless dark might still have hope in the ungodly things we do to each other in it.

[Relics of hate scattered working-class
parts of city. When will we become
our own rivers and rage like so many
angry bees?]

The Translations

1

All the overpriced concert tickets
    in the world, all the maternal warnings
of my childhood not to wear those 1970s
    headphones: it might worsen
the nerve
                        damage, violence done
                                (half-deaf
but not disabled)
                      by a Meningitis
that swept into my body like a song sweeps

through a movie scene, somehow making it more
    meaningful. Without the disease, I would just
be white, almost translucent. I wouldn't be able to
    reflect back at the sun
that there's
                    something about me,
                            too. That the streets
I live on
                    have buried musical bones, whose percussion
against the asphalt keeps me from a quiet life in my head

that's never been anything but a 6ᵗʰ Street, where
    I slide along the sides of stages holding a stranger's
hand, and he's the one because the bass
    vibrates my entire body until it tingles and doesn't
resemble my body
                  at all but feels
                            as though I've slid on
someone else's skin
                  as simply as putting on a dress—
maybe a shimmy over my hips.

2

I'm singing but it's someone else's voice.
    This happens in the shower, in the car, in
conversation. Some people wear masks; I wear
    songs. They can hang in my throat for days
or weeks, whole
                 albums looping in my mouth
                            until they've been
assigned memories.
                 Four-minute photographs. Even
regular noises can pass for music if I let them.

And sometimes spoken words are so muffled
    I must imagine they are part of a song.
Someone's humming in my good
    ear, something about being healed. But I
kind of enjoy
                 not understanding what everyone
                        is saying all the time,
so maybe don't bother
                 taking me to a witch doctor or a priest
who thinks that a sweaty hand and a prayer can help

me hear everything. I thought I'd be sick from receiving
    holy water that who knows how many people had dipped
fingers in. And all those wheelchairs squealing, voices
    muffling into each other, an old man clearing
and clearing
                 and clearing his throat—
                       they had to become
music for me to make it through.

3

So many voices inside me that haven't even
    been heard yet. Outlets with mouths
open, ready themselves for me to stick
    wet fingers in them, to welcome the shock
of not having to be
                    me for a while. And it's really
                            okay that I absorbed
those headphones all their years
                    because the way I hear hasn't changed—
I listen with my whole body to the songs beating me

awake from dreams with their drums, their sliding
    notes, their off-keys, their Dear Prudences,
their fade-outs like tangles with wasps.
    The way the slow ones make me cry no matter what
the lyrics are telling me.
                    The way the right beat
                            can even make a Baptist
find the dance floor
                    because music is the finger-
wagging Lord, the story-telling Jesus, and most of all,

the Judas who kisses the cheek softly before metal-mouthing
    to the people who are sure they already knew
all there is to know. Don't trust anyone who doesn't
    listen to music. Even the fully deaf can appreciate
vibrations and pulses.
                    What I meant to say was:
                            don't trust anyone
who cannot allow music to suck them deep,
                    the way I've always wanted some god to
suck me into epic darkness, the kind with designs,

the kind in which the blood of ancient
    banjoing fingers
flows from strings,
    where even fibers of muscles
can create sound.
                But I can't play or at least
                      try hard enough. All I can do is
open my mouth
            and sing to a heaven I don't believe in anymore,
but I do believe in other things.

Dear
    all I've never
heard, music
    I'm maybe addressing:
don't you want to sing
           more than my sins?

[In order to find the language
of all things, we must walk
down the street, not be so
busy eating our hearts out
in the marketplace.]

To Tinnitus

O, susurrus, you've
stood me up in stiff
ear bones, left me paper
wings that rats will eat
before I know to know
it's time to leave.

When these cricket
cities inside cannot
drown out a girl not as
loved as lies they told
one another, then the film
in which I should've been

is the silent kind,
campy pantomime
of gorilla suit and girl:
hands on face, dodges
the chase, and never stops
to wash fur from her teeth.

To All the Sheep on Conic Hill, Balmaha

You shouldn't have crowded this biped to near
imbalance but given me time and space to find
my footing because busting my face on a rock's sharp

edge in front of boys is not any kind of lullaby.
Besides that, who knows (you know) how much
of Conic's mud is actually mud? I know your type:

look as harmless as fireflies as you dot the hillside
with your yellowed wool, but really you were quite
pissed we were up there taking up space at your

dinner table as though we had the right to tromp
over it, plant a flag at its highest point. I noticed
how you mocked my slow thigh muscles with your

deliberate chewing, and as the flock of you filtered
downhill to get on home for the night, you paused
to stare us down. We had no numbers spray-painted

on our backs. Soundless, we filed down the muddy way
out of June mist; sometimes, I can feel your eyes press
against my body like the springs of an old mattress.

[Shake off the language
of eyes smoking like fresh guns,
but give it a goddamn name.]

Ninsun to the Deities after Her Son Gilgamesh's Death

Don't expect me to graze any longer
in your backward thinking. I'm no virgin, no
whore but a wild cow who chokes

on the grass you've grown in this pasture.
Carnivorous now—I crave only the ghost
flesh of gods who are always burying

something, who allow any myth to move
mouths. *Taste like this. Be this.* There is
no music to set this mood, but I dream

of a young composer who can siphon
revenge to her notes—a song to an
unfaithful lover still loved, still loved even

though he's beaten himself out of a woman's
heart like a drum beats out war. Except this beating
cannot just belong to a heart—it's not strong

enough to contain all of this longing,
neither are the sun nor moon that buff
clueless faces on this unkind earth.

When you were piling up silt and dredging
rivers, did you give any thought to what it
might birth? You must've forgotten that—

in the adrenaline rush that creation brings—
you set into motion a season of last songs
driven away by nightjars without homes.

Self-Portrait as a Boy in *A Musician Family*

(ca. 1828, Francois-Joseph Navez)

My papa told me to keep a sparrow
in my shirt pocket all day as we travel
to the next town plaza to perform, and
when the moon stares me down, to listen
to the songs she writes while others sleep.

He says this will make me a musician,
that birdsong is key to understanding
where the chords come from.
So far, I am still cursed with clumsy fingers,
and *No ear*, papa says, but as I listen, I forget

I can hate myself when mama makes
the mandolin slur, as papa hammers on
the violin for the crowd's favorite tarantella,
when sister twirls—a spider on its safety rope.
I'm full of everything and nothing

like my suitcase, like the hoop my dog jumps
through and through, and this sparrow
worries me: what if her voice fails, what if
she falls, what if I can't let her go? Is there
language to find in the folds of shadow

with which to eulogize? When I sleep,
I dream that she suffocates. I feed her
to my dog who's had nothing to eat;
papa stares at me with distant eyes,
as though he is just sleepwalking, but says

nothing. Awake again, I'm just trying to hear
my way out of moments. I call out for
Apollo, who, even if he does not make out
my words, might sense that I'm afraid
that the sky cannot always contain the music.

Until the Bees

Everyone is investigated.
Even the bees in their

slacking off, sloughing off
this world. Scientists say,

when the bees go, all of us
will take our last breath

together in unmarked
cemeteries. That's why

I touch your face that way—
to understand the language

that trembles those pools
before our tendons and

bones are gnawed bare
enough to be cilia in swamps.

I used to say I'd put our lives
in honey, enjoy the slowdown

in our own sweet time.
But time isn't what's squeezing.

It's these bodies that are next
to each other, minds apart;

these cement-mixer mouths;
these hands that buzz with

uneasiness as executors of
this isle of doom. We pull

stingers from our flesh,
toothpaste the swelling red—

the only obsession left,
until finally, the bees.

['Could tune that devil in us with the heel of hate.
'Could be fools for these unholy hands
that'd start a war or fill our throats with cement
just so that some blues are never recorded.]

Songs from Terezín

Prelude

You think that this is somebody
else's wound, that because you don't see
these walls in the act of crumbling, they
are done with all of that. This flake of wall

is not unlike how you slough off skin, though
history falling lightly to the ground doesn't
want to be revitalized like a useful organ.
It isn't better for these walls to come down,

but better that there's a change in your face
when the sunlight catches the long row
of gleaming white sinks. Still shine. Still hover
around the grim peace that's made a home.

1

Sing through
the black and white film
on your eyes. Sing
for the milk money.
Sing as though your belly
doesn't ache. Sing
until you become
the bumblebee.
Then sting.

2

This kind of blues is sung only under
the worst conditions when *we* and *they*
are so far apart that we can pretend
the others' music disintegrates on its way
to our ears. None of this is firsthand.
But you can still feel the music of this place
as though words were being pulled through
your throat like a heavy rope that
all of the dead hang onto via the knot
outside of your body. Music is exile.
If you can't hear it to know as much, no one
ever called your name: skin of the Earth.

3

Within this barbed wire,
oh, so many flies could bloom,
hidden away inside our skin.

4

They walk away from the camera
as if to say: *pick our bones, they're
almost clean*; the meantime makes
musical instruments of their bodies,

orchestras the Nazis cannot hear.
The percussion still in their bellies,
they rile up the nameless something
on which their bodies must survive.

5

Even the man
was just a man
playing the mustache
on a man:
organ grinder.

6

Two barn swallows with their forked tails
fly around the peeling walls to get to their
single nest; they are reluctant to spit-shine
the mud and straw in which they make
a life. This way of living is not propaganda.
Stand in this room alone with the birds
for too long and begin to picture them
here in greater numbers until mud nests take
up all the empty space of a wall but don't
have the physical strength to take it down.

7

Arbeit macht frei.

Roll this city toward you.
Roll it like the syllables of a new
language over your tongue.

Hudba tě osvobodí.

Listen!

The heaviest wheel
Rolls across our foreheads
To bury itself.

8

Mattresses stuffed with sheet music,
walls spilled over with the energy
of souls not ready to be done
with life, brass and strings
smuggled into a city of last breaths
of which you can still feel the legato,
one song rising up and on, turning,
twisting in our heads like a jazz
that, for one more composition,
one more measure, one more god-
damned clear note, will make us shine.

Coda

Body close to body
clanging
like the bells that wake us
from our dreams.

NOTES

The vignettes in brackets throughout the book are based on the music and research on the life of Huddie William Ledbetter, Leadbelly, and are influenced by the work of Rachel Eliza Griffiths, Jake Adam York, Martha Collins, Yusef Komunyakaa, and Tyehimba Jess.

"Big Thicket Blues"

Texas' Big Thicket National Preserve is the landscape of my childhood. It is also where James Byrd, Jr. was dragged to his death on June 7, 1998 at the age of 49. Quoted portions of the poem are from various news reports and interviews, and some information on Byrd is from the documentary titled *Byrd: The Life and Tragic Death of James Byrd, Jr.* (2008). Various lyrics, which are represented in italics throughout the poem, are by The National, Irene Cara, Fleet Foxes, Al Green, and Prince. Thanks to Jake Adam York's "An Unfinished Sentence," Yusef Komunyakaa's "Autobiography of My Alter Ego," and C.D. Wright's recent works, *One Big Self* and *One with Others,* for showing me that I had no choice but to write this poem.

"Asena, the Gray Wolf, to Tu Kuëh, after Many Years"

This poem is based on a Turkish myth in which a boy, Tu Kuëh, becomes the sole surviving member of a Turkish clan, is left legless and armless in a ditch by ruthless conquerors, and is rescued and raised by Asena, a she-wolf. According to the myth, the man and wolf eventually beget the entire Ottoman Empire and reside in the valley of a metal mountain range, the Altais, until Asena leads them out of the valley to conquer.

"Clamorous Pauses Between Marquees and Parking Lots"

This title is borrowed from Lynda Hull's "Gateway to Manhattan," and the first line is from "Midnight Reports." Both are from her collection, *Star Ledger*.

"Throat Circus"

This poem is inspired by Malinda Markham's collection, *Having Cut the Sparrow's Heart*.

"The Translations"

Thanks to Lynda Hull's poem about Charlie Parker, "Ornithology," whose structure I borrowed and from which I drew inspiration for this poem. Thanks also to Oliver Sacks' *Seeing Voices* and the eight million hearing exams I endured throughout elementary school.

"Ninsun to the Deities after Gilgamesh's Death"

Ninsun ("Lady Wild Cow") is a Sumerian goddess and mother of Gilgamesh; she interprets his dreams and asks the gods for her son's protection on his journey. Thanks to Herbert Mason's translation of the *Gilgamesh* epic.

"Self-Portrait as a Boy in *A Musician Family*"

Thanks to the National Galleries of Scotland in Edinburgh where Navez's oil painting, *A Musician Family*, is housed.

"Songs from Terezín"

Terezín is a concentration camp outside of Prague, Czech Republic, to which the Nazis sent many Jewish musicians and composers during World War II. Though not considered a "death camp," thousands of men, women, and children died from malnutrition and disease while they were there, and many more were eventually transported to Auschwitz to be murdered. Hitler tried to hide what he considered "degenerate music" inside the walls of Terezín. This poem contains references to *Brundibár* (*Bumblebee*), a children's opera performed at Terezín and composed by Jewish Czech, Hans Krása; poems, which are preserved in the Terezin Museum, by some of the children who were interred at the camp; and the propaganda documentary made by Nazis to disguise the horrors of the camp for the benefit of the Red Cross and the world, *Terezin: A Documentary Film from the Jewish Settlement Area* (1944). Translations—*Arbeit Macht Frei* (German): "Work sets you free;" *Hudba tě osvobodí* (Czech): "Music sets you free."

Section titles "First the Bodies, Then the Names" and "A Jukebox or a Coffin" (altered in my version), and the poem title, "No Condoms for the Heart," are partial quotes from C.D. Wright's *One Big Self*. I hope her words will always buzz under our skin. Hive them.

THANKS

Thanks to Zachary Green for knowing the kind of space I needed to finish this book. So much gratitude: for unflappable mentors, William Olsen and Nancy Eimers; for Cynthia Klekar and Cynthia Running-Johnson; for editor and dear friend, Beth Marzoni; for poem-a-day collaborator, Michael Levan; for their humbling commentary, Tyehimba Jess, TJ Jarrett, and Ailish Hopper; for his guidance and poem/blurb, Mark Turcotte; for family, friends, and former colleagues who've supported this writing in so many ways; for their dedication to making this book so damn beautiful, the Sundress team, especially Erin Elizabeth Smith, Kristen Ton, and Jane Huffman; and for The Graduate College at Western Michigan University for a Gwen Frostic Fellowship that allowed me the time to finish an earlier version of this manuscript.

ABOUT THE AUTHOR

Originally from small-town Southeast Texas, Natalie Giarratano received her Ph.D. in creative writing from Western Michigan University. She is the author of *Leaving Clean* (Briery Creek Press, 2013), which won the 2013 Liam Rector First Book Prize in Poetry. Her poems have appeared in *Sakura Review, Black Tongue Review, Beltway Poetry, Tupelo Quarterly, Tinderbox,* and *TYPO,* among others. She edits and lives in Northern Colorado with her partner, their daughter, and pup.

OTHER SUNDRESS TITLES

Babbage's Dream
Neil Aitken
$15

Posada: Offerings of Witness and Refuge
Xochitl Julisa Bermejo
$15

At Whatever Front
Les Kay
$15

No More Milk
Karen Craigo
$15

Theater of Parts
M. Mack
$15

Suites for the Modern Dancer
Jill Khoury
$15

Every Love Story is an Apocalypse Story
Donna Vorreyer
$14

What Will Keep Us Alive
Kristin LaTour
$14

Ha Ha Ha Thump
Amorak Huey
$14

Stationed Near the Gateway
Margaret Bashaar
$14

major characters in minor films
Kristy Bowen
$14

Confluence
Sandra Marchetti
$14

Hallelujah for the Ghosties
Melanie Jordan
$14

Fortress
Kristina Marie Darling
$14

When I Wake It Will Be Forever
Virginia Smith Rice
$14

A House of Many Windows
Donna Vorreyer
$14

The Hardship Post
Jehanne Dubrow
$14

One Perfect Bird
Letitia Trent
$14

Like a Fish
Daniel Crocker
$14

The Bone Folders
T.A. Noonan
$14

CPSIA information can be obtained
at www.ICGtesting.com
Printed in the USA
FSOW03n0313070817
37162FS